THE LITTLE LOVE BOOK

Also by Giles Andreae

PURPLE RONNIE'S BOOK OF LOVE
PURPLE RONNIE'S GUIDE TO LIFE
THE SMASHING WORLD OF PURPLE RONNIE
PURPLE RONNIE'S STAR SIGNS
LOVE POEMS BY PURPLE RONNIE
THE VERY BEST OF PURPLE RONNIE
WHAT IS LOVE?

THE LITTLE LOVE BOOK

Giles Andreae

Illustrations by
Janet Cronin

To my brothers Simon, Hugo and Tobyn
and to Janet's parents, Joseph and Marianna

ISBN: 0 340 62841 3
Printed and bound in Great Britain by
Mackays of Chatham PLC, Chatham, Kent

Hodder and Stoughton Ltd
A division of Hodder Headline PLC
338 Euston Road
London NW1 3BH

Contents:

WHERE DOES LOVE COME FROM?

Love is in everything all over the world.

In the rocks, the trees and the rivers . . .

. . . in the animals and in the people.

But some people still spend their whole time looking for love . . .

. . . while others seem to be stuffed full of it all the time.

The problem is,
the more time you
spend looking for love . . .

. . . the less you are
likely to find it.

Because finding love
starts with giving it,
not with trying to get it.

And once we start giving love there is no
telling where it will end.

Love is what binds our world together

and love is what makes it work

HOW DOES LOVE WORK?

There are three
different ways of
loving.

Living in love

Falling in love

and <u>Being</u> in love.

LIVING IN LOVE

When we live in love we try to make the world around us a better place.

People who live in love bring everything to life.

Living in love
means doing
things rather
than waiting
for them to
happen.

People who do not live in love
will find it very difficult to fall in love.

FALLING IN LOVE

When we are children the world seems to be full of magic and miracles.

But when we grow up we often forget how exciting our lives could be.

Falling in love is what happens when two people open each other up to the magic of the world again.

When you fall in love you feel dizzy with happiness, your body buzzes with attraction . . .

. . . and you want to stroke, hug and kiss each other all the time.

But when you fall in love it is not just each other's love that you are feeling . . .

. . . but your own love, directed through each other, onto the whole of the world.

BEING IN LOVE

Being in love is what happens after the thrill of falling in love calms down . . .

. . . and you decide that you believe in each other enough to commit yourselves to loving each other for longer.

Falling in love is a powerful explosion of feelings and desires.

Being in love is a calm state of committed love and friendship.

WHO SHOULD WE LOVE?

Some people believe that it is possible to find the perfect partner.

That out of all the millions of people on the planet there is someone somewhere who is exactly right for each of us.

But if we wait for the right person to love,
we might end up not loving anyone at all.

The best way to fall in love is not to wait for someone special . . .

. . . but to live in love with everyone . . . all the time.

WHO DO WE FALL IN LOVE WITH?

As we grow up we begin to find certain things in people attractive . . .

. . . or ugly.

We start to
know what we
need from
people . . .

. . . and what
we can give
to them.

The more loving we are, the more people we are likely to be open to.

And when we find someone who fits what we know about ourselves . .

. . . we fall in love.

LOVE AND BEAUTY

When people
fall in love,
they find each
other
beautiful.

And although some people think that
beauty is about what your body looks
like . . .

Lovers know
that beauty is
not about what
you are like
<u>outside</u> . . .

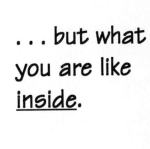

. . . but what
you are like
<u>inside</u>.

In fact, lovers often see beauty in each other that other people can never see themselves.

WHAT DOES LOVE FEEL LIKE?

ooh, it's all sort of warm and gooey and lonely!

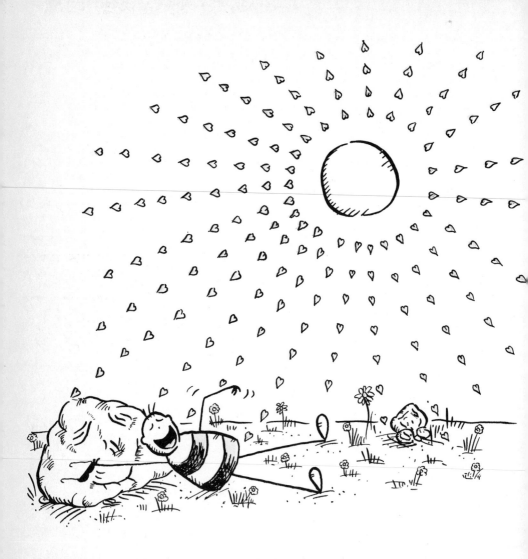

People often think that love is a feeling.
Like feeling hot or cold, happy or sad,
hungry or full.

Certainly when you first <u>fall</u> in love you have all sorts of feelings . . .

. . . often all at the same time.

But what should we do when these feelings start to fade away?

Some people just move on to the next relationship . . .

... and the next ...

... and the next ...

... without really finding love at all.

If love were just a feeling then it could go away just as easily as it comes . . .

. . . and we would never be able to make choices about who we love at all.

Love is not a feeling
but a decision to be
there for someone.

Love is a commitment to use your actions,
your thoughts and your words to support
each other as much as you can.

phew!

There will always be good and bad feelings, happiness and sadness in every loving relationship.

But when love unfolds as a commitment, the strength, the pleasure and the depth of it is there for everyone to see.

MAKING LOVE

Love is not something that we <u>feel</u>.
Love is something that we <u>make</u>.

When we give love we receive it.

And the more love we
receive, the more we
<u>want</u> to give.

So that the world's
love builds . . .

. . . and builds

. . . and builds.

THE RULES OF LOVE

If we want to continue loving throughout the whole of our lives, there are several rules which we must learn.

LOVE IS TRUSTING

Some people see the world as a cold and hostile place full of traps and pitfalls.

But Loving People see it as a friendly and joyful environment full of wonder, surprise and opportunity.

People who build
walls around
themselves may
be closed away
from being hurt.

But they are
closed away
from being
loved as well.

Loving people know that if we are open, honest and trusting towards other people . . .

. . . they are likely to open up to us as well.

LOVE IS BEING OURSELVES

Some people believe they love each other when they cannot do anything separately or bear to be apart.

But Loving People let others be who they
want to be . . .

. . . and help them grow towards their own
individual goals.

Loving People recognise that our happiness does not depend upon other people . . .

. . . but upon ourselves.

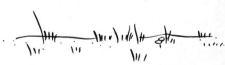

It is our own uniqueness that makes us all different from one another.

And it is these differences that make us loveable.

Love is Communication

Some people think that they always know what others are thinking . . .

. . . so never stop to listen to what they might say.

But Loving People know that love means listening to each other without judgement . . .

. . . and talking openly and honestly about our feelings however hard it might be.

If we take the time to put ourselves in each other's places and see things how someone else sees them . . .

. . . we can often come to understand each other much more fully.

Love is Playfulness

Some people think that playing is only for children.

But Loving People know that playfulness is the best way we have to celebrate our love for each other.

Worrying about the past or fantasising about the future can often mean that we have no time left for loving in the present.

Playfulness gives us a way of living in love right now.

Playing's not so much fun
on your own

Love is Spontaneity

Sometimes people get into habits which stop them from keeping their love alive.

Loving People know that making changes and organising surprises shows that we never take our love for granted.

Love is Encouragement

Some people prefer to bring attention to the weaknesses of others rather than to parise their strengths.

But Loving People know that you only get the best out of people if you let them know how much confidence you have in them.

A FINAL WORD

Love is the most important thing we have in the world.

Let us use it all we can.